ANIMAL FAMILIES
Elephants

General Editor
Tim Harris

WAYLAND

WAYLAND

This edition published in 2014 by Wayland

Copyright © 2014 Brown Bear Books Ltd.

Wayland
Hachette Children's Books
338 Euston Road
London NW1 3BH

Wayland Australia
Level 17/207 Kent Street
Sydney, NSW 2000

All Rights Reserved.

Brown Bear Books Ltd.
First Floor
9–17 St. Albans Place
London
N1 0NX

Managing Editor: Tim Harris
Designer: Lynne Lennon
Picture Manager: Sophie Mortimer
Art Director: Jeni Child
Production Director: Alastair Gourlay
Editorial Director: Lindsey Lowe
Children's Publisher: Anne O'Daly

ISBN: 978-0-7502-8452-3

Printed in China

10 9 8 7 6 5 4 3 2 1

Wayland is a division of Hachette Children's Books,
an Hachette UK company.
www.hachette.co.uk

Websites

Picture Credits

Contents

Introduction

Elephants are the biggest and strongest of all land-living animals. With their trunks, tusks and giant ears, they look like no other animal.

As well as being powerful, elephants are intelligent. They have large brains that grow through youth, making them very good at learning. In fact, they display some behaviour seen in few other animals.

Elephants are mammals, like we are. They make caring mothers, showing great care towards their young. There are two different types (species) of elephants. One type lives in Africa, and the other lives in Asia.

The African elephant is the largest land animal. Its long trunk and large ears make it unmistakable.

Using tools

Elephants often use tools. Wild elephants have been seen using twigs and branches to brush away flies or scratch themselves. Elephants are the only animals apart from monkeys and other primates that can throw things. Using their trunk like an arm, they sometimes pick up objects and hurl them at other animals or people.

Elephants are social animals. They all spend at least part of their lives in groups. Some elephants never leave the groups they were born into.

In this book you will learn all about how elephants live together. Later on you will find out more about just what makes them such special animals.

This Asian elephant has just used its trunk to suck up some water for a drink.

The elephant's trunk

An elephant's trunk is a combination of its nose and its upper lip. It contains lots of different muscles, making it flexible and easy to manoeuvre. Elephants use their trunks to pick up food, suck up water, caress one another, fight, smell and make trumpeting calls.

Elephant herds

Most elephants live in groups called herds. The basic elephant herd is an extended family of female elephants and their young.

Adult male (called bull) elephants usually live alone, but sometimes they live in temporary herds of their own. They only join the female herds when they are looking for a mate. The females in the basic elephant herd are always related. They spend their whole lives together, and the bonds between them are strong. They help each other raise and protect the young, they travel together, and they feed as a group. Herd members rarely move more than 15 metres (50 ft) apart.

Big and small herds

African elephant herds range from two to about 24 animals. Sometimes herds of related female elephants join to form groups of 50 or so members, called clans. Asian elephants have smaller herds of usually ten or fewer animals. If herds get too big, they split in two.

◀ **Female elephants with their calves. Most females in a herd are related, and they help each other care for the young.**

These herds often meet, with a lot of excitement and friendly trumpeting noises. Elephant herds do not always stay in the same place, but each does have certain areas where it can often be found. These areas may be shared with other herds.

The leader of the herd

The leader of the herd is the matriarch. She is the oldest and largest female. She makes decisions that affect the others. The matriarch leads the herd to find new feeding grounds. When she stops to feed, the rest of the herd stops with her.

Adult and calf Asian elephants have a cooling bathe in a river. Bathing is a favourite activity for elephants.

Washing off and dusting down

Elephants enjoy bathing. When they reach a river or watering hole, they often wade right in before even taking a drink. Bathing cleans the skin and cools the elephants. It also gives youngsters an excuse to play.

Staying in touch

Elephants are great communicators. With their trunks and huge ears they have very good senses of smell and hearing. They use both to keep in touch.

Elephants can 'talk' to each other over very long distances. They can send messages across several kilometres (miles) using infrasound (see the box). They use normal sound and infrasound to communicate at closer range.

Body language

When they can see each other, elephants use body language, touch and smell much more. The ears are used like flags. They are spread out to show aggression or dominance and flattened back against the head to indicate submission or fear. The trunk is also used for communication. When two elephants meet

➔ **Two male elephants greet each other by gently touching their trunks.**

after being apart, one puts its trunk into the other's mouth as a greeting. Swinging the trunk forwards is a threat. Mothers comfort their infants by touching them with their trunks.

Elephants have a very good sense of smell. They raise their trunks and sniff the air to get information about their surroundings. They recognise different members of the herd by their odour, and they can smell elephants from outside the herd too. They may even be able to tell when another elephant is becoming excited or angry by changes in its odour.

Jungle rumbles

As well as making trumpeting noises, elephants use very low-pitched sounds, called infrasound, to 'talk' to each other. Infrasound is too low-pitched for humans to hear ('infra' means below). But for a large animal like an elephant the sound is easy to pick up. Elephants use infrasound to communicate over long distances.

⬦ **Communication is an important part of elephant society. It helps adults and calves stay together.**

Getting enough to eat

A fully grown bull African elephant can weigh 7.3 tonnes (8 tons) – the weight of 100 people. That makes finding enough food each day a full-time job.

An adult male elephant eats up to 159 kilograms (350 lbs) of plant matter every day. He can spend 18 hours a day looking for it. An elephant can eat a wide range of plants and it can feed at many different levels. This helps the elephant get all the food it needs.

Having a long trunk makes it easy for elephants to reach up high for food. They also pick up fallen fruit from the ground.

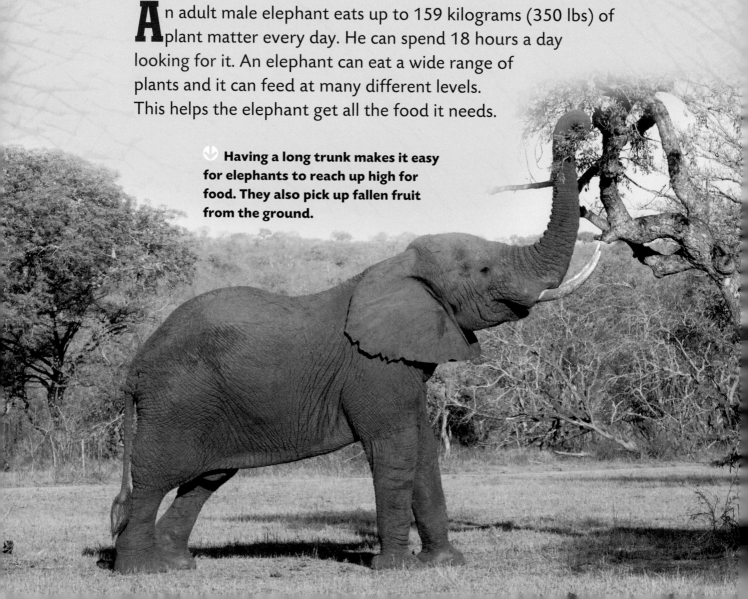

Drinking

Elephants drink a lot of water. An adult African elephant can drink up to 190 litres (50 gallons) a day. An elephant sucks water into its trunk then squirts it into its mouth. Herds usually travel to water at least once a day but can go without it for two weeks.

Elephants prefer some watering holes to others. They choose those with high amounts of minerals in the water.

Using its trunk, it can tear grass from the ground or reach up to strip leaves from the high branches of trees. It can also rip away tree bark that it has loosened with its tusks.

Eat, eat, eat

Once it has grasped the food with its trunk, an elephant passes the food up to its mouth. There, four huge teeth called molars (two in each jaw) crush and grind the food before the animal swallows. Food takes between 22 and 46 hours to pass through the body as dung. Elephant dung provides food for many smaller animals and is also excellent fertiliser for the soil.

Elephants need so much food that they spend nearly every waking hour feeding. The herd munches through much of the day and most of the night as well. True sleep is just two or three hours around the hottest time of the day or just after midnight.

The mating game

When a female elephant is about 10 or 11 years old, she is able to mate for the first time. She is then said to be 'in estrus'.

Females in estrus attract nearby males to mate with them. When a female starts to come into estrus, she often walks in an unusual way. She holds her head high and looks back over her shoulders. This is called an estrus walk, and it may help draw males to her. Females in estrus also make special sounds. Some of these sounds can be heard by humans; others are too low. These sounds may help attract roaming males.

A bull elephant 'in must' dribbles oily liquid from glands behind his eyes.

Males 'in must'

About once every year adult bull elephants go through a change in their behaviour known as must. Must is caused by increased levels of the male hormone, testosterone. Bulls 'in must' are much more aggressive than usual, and other bulls usually keep away from them. When two 'must bulls' meet, they often end up fighting each other.

A male and a female Asian elephant twist their trunks around each other. They do this before they mate.

Before mating takes place

Once she has attracted a bull elephant, the female usually urinates. She does this so that the male can smell the odour of her urine. The odour tells the bull whether the female is really ready to mate or not. If she is ready, he becomes excited. The female walks quickly away, and the bull chases after her. Female elephants are quicker than males, so if she is not impressed by her partner, she can easily get away from him. If she does like him, she will let him catch up with her, and the pair will then mate. The largest bull elephants are most popular with females. Bull elephants that are in must are always chosen rather than those that are not in must.

Asian elephants have a slightly different mating behaviour from African elephants. Asian elephants stand face to face and twine their trunks together before they mate.

Bringing up the calves

Baby elephants, or calves, can walk within an hour, but they are very shaky on their feet for the first few days. The mother stays close to her baby.

The mother feeds the young elephant on her milk and protects it from enemies for the first year of its life. The other females in the herd help to bring up the baby. If the mother is separated from her calf for any reason, one of the other females rushes to its side to comfort it. These elephant 'aunts' will even let a youngster comfort-suckle.

Play time

When they are not feeding or travelling with the herd, baby elephants spend a lot of time playing. They charge playfully at smaller animals, birds and bushes, and they jostle with each other.
Young males spend a lot of time wrestling and

↩ **Elephant calves spend much of their time playing – particularly with each other.**

Growing up

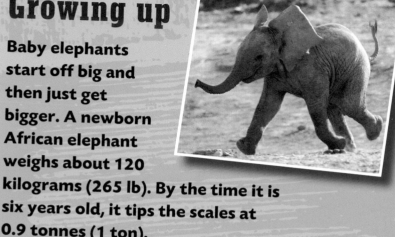

Baby elephants start off big and then just get bigger. A newborn African elephant weighs about 120 kilograms (265 lb). By the time it is six years old, it tips the scales at 0.9 tonnes (1 ton).

An adult sprays water over a calf to keep it cool. An elephant's trunk can hold up to 5.7 litres (10 pints) of water.

chasing one another around. As they get older, they find new partners for these games. By the time they are six or seven years old they start leaving the herd for short periods. They search for different families to find males of a similar age to play-fight with.

Young females

Young females gradually grow out of play. At five or six years old they start helping to care for the smallest babies. They keep an eye on them while the mother is busy and sometimes guard them while they sleep.

Male elephants

Young male elephants start to become adults when they are about 12. Their play gets more aggressive, and they spend more time away from the herd.

Young males finally leave the herd when they are 15 or 16. As they get more aggressive, the older females lose patience. Eventually the females drive the young elephants away from the herd. Once they have left, male elephants behave in different ways. Some wander by themselves, while others form all-male groups. A few join a different family

Two bulls clash in a head-to-head fight. A battle between bulls can last up to six hours!

herd. They stay with it for up to a year then go off on their own.

While they are in their late teens and early twenties, bull elephants keep the herding instinct. They join large groups of females for short periods or travel with other bulls. All-male herds are good places for the younger bull elephants to test out their strength.

All by himself

Fully grown bulls wander from herd to herd, particularly when they are looking for a female to mate with. As bull elephants get older, they spend more time on their own. The oldest bulls usually live alone. Most stay near swamps where there is water and vegetation soft enough to chew with their worn-out teeth.

Adult male elephants spend some time with a herd and some time alone.

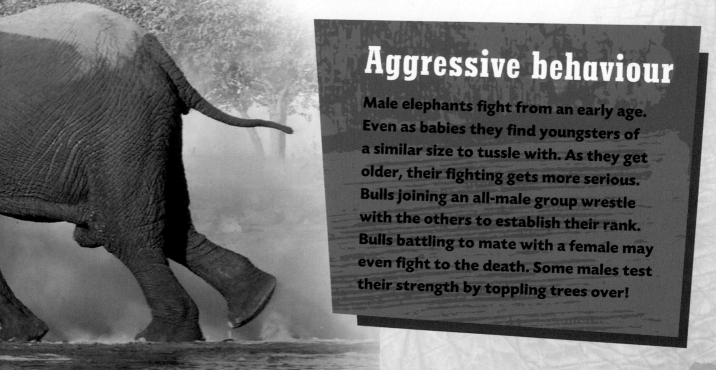

Aggressive behaviour

Male elephants fight from an early age. Even as babies they find youngsters of a similar size to tussle with. As they get older, their fighting gets more serious. Bulls joining an all-male group wrestle with the others to establish their rank. Bulls battling to mate with a female may even fight to the death. Some males test their strength by toppling trees over!

Female elephants

Females spend their whole lives in the family groups they were born into. When they are a few years old, they play less and help out more.

Eventually, female elephants attract the attention of adult males. Females first mate when they are 10 or 11 years old. Once she has mated, a female carries her unborn baby growing inside her for more than 22 months. The bonding between females in the elephant herd is strong. Most herds are extended family groups, and all the females in them are

⬇ **Adult elephants gather around calves to protect them when danger threatens.**

closely related. Because they are all either mothers, daughters, sisters or cousins of one another, they work together to look after the young.

⬆ **A mother stays close to her calf for the whole of its first year. Other females will also help out.**

The protection of the herd

When a mother is busy feeding, a younger female watches over her baby to make sure it does not get into difficulties. When faced by a predator, the whole herd forms a wall of trunks and legs to shield the infants. It must be a menacing sight for a would-be attacker.

Female elephants never grow as big as the adult males, nor do they grow such long tusks. Female Asian elephants hardly have tusks at all.

Birth

Females have their first baby when they are 12 or 13. Some give birth surrounded by the rest of the herd. Others leave for a short while to have the baby alone. Elephants give birth standing up, so babies have a big drop to the ground!

When elephants grow old and die

Elephants are among the longest-lived of all animals. Wild African elephants can easily reach 60 years old, and wild Asian elephants may live to 70.

Because of their size adult elephants have very few predators. Diseases kill some elephants when they are still young, but many live to old age. Starvation is the main natural killer of elephants. Every elephant gets six sets of very large molar teeth in its lifetime. Once the sixth set has worn out, the elephant can no longer feed, so it starves to death.

Poaching and shooting

Apart from starvation the main killer of elephants is humans. Many African elephants never get to reach a natural death. One reason for this is because they are poached for their ivory tusks.

⤶ These playful young elephants could live for another 50 years or more.

Several African elephants sniff the bones of a dead elephant.

Another reason is that some are shot to prevent their numbers growing too large. Asian elephants are not hunted in the same way, so most live to old age.

Understanding death?

Elephants do some things that suggest they may understand death. Whenever they come across dead elephants, they become excited. They explore the bones with their trunks and even pick them up.

Elephant graves

There are places where lots of elephant skeletons have been found together. Sick and dying elephants usually go to areas where there is plenty of food and water. The elephants die there, and their bones collect over the years.

There are places like this in Africa and Asia where elephants go to die.

Ears, tusks and trunks

With its long trunk, enormous ears and tusks an elephant looks like nothing else on Earth. Each of these strange things has an important job to do.

Why are an elephant's ears so big? The main reason is that they help elephants cool down. Each ear is filled with hundreds of blood vessels. As the blood flows through the vessels in the ear, heat escapes through the skin into the surrounding air. When the weather gets really hot, elephants often flap their ears, which helps them lose heat even more quickly.

Strong teeth

The tusks are giant incisor teeth. Elephants use their tusks to pull up roots, tear the bark off trees and dig out waterholes. They also use their tusks as weapons. Elephants come in different sizes. An adult bull African elephant may weigh 6.4 tonnes (7 tons) and stand 3.6 metres (12 ft) tall.

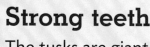 **It is easy to tell an Asian elephant, such as this one, from its African cousin. Asian elephants have smaller ears and a domed head. Their bodies are smaller and chunkier.**

Trunks

An African elephant has two 'fingers' at the end of its trunk (left), while an Asian elephant has one (right).

⬇ An African bush elephant's ears make up one seventh of its body surface.

Elephant ancestors

Elephants have lived on Earth for around 50 million years. The earliest elephant (*Moenitherium*) was about the size of a pig and had no trunk.

It was another 15 million years before creatures that we might recognise as elephants first appeared. *Phimia* lived 35 million years ago. This early elephant had a short trunk and tusks coming from both its upper and lower jaws.

Mastadons and mammoths

One of the later elephant species was *Platybelodon*. This strange-looking creature lived about 20 million years ago in marshy areas. It used its shovel-shaped teeth to dig up vegetation. Another early elephant was the now-extinct mastodon. Mastodons looked like the modern Asian elephant and the woolly mammoth, but they were not closely related to them. Mastodons first appeared long before either mammoths or modern elephants evolved.

⬇ **The earliest elephants looked nothing like their modern relatives. As elephants evolved (changed over time), they began to look more like the animals we know today. They developed trunks and tusks.**

Moenitherium

Phimia

The woolly mammoth was a large elephant with long, sharply curved tusks. It was covered with a shaggy coat of hair to keep it warm in the frozen lands where it lived. Our own ancestors hunted woolly mammoths for food until they died out about 10,000 years ago. Mammoths were more closely related to the Asian elephant than to the African elephant.

Elephants in America

Elephants now live only in Africa and Asia. But once there were relatives of elephants in Europe and America. Mammoths lived in England until about 14,000 years ago, and mastodons lived in America until 10,000 years ago. Mammoths lived mainly on the plains and mastodons mainly in the forests. They died out because the climate changed and because people hunted them.

⬆ **Hyraxes are among elephants' closest living relatives. They are rabbit-sized animals with hooves.**

Platybelodon

Mammoth

Elephant habitats

Elephants live in a variety of different types of environment. The African savanna elephant lives mostly on dry open plains and in open woodland.

The African forest elephant and Asian elephant are creatures of thick tropical forests. Elephants are tough animals. In Africa they live in scorching desert and near the chilly peaks of mountains as high as 4,572 metres (15,000 feet). All they need to survive is enough food to eat and water to drink.

Africa and Asia

About 100 years ago African elephants roamed across the whole of Africa south of the Sahara Desert. They followed ancient paths in search of food and water. Asian elephants lived from the

Shrinking homelands

The main threat to elephants in the wild is habitat destruction. As the human population has grown, so has the demand for farmland. The red areas on the map (right) show where elephants still live.

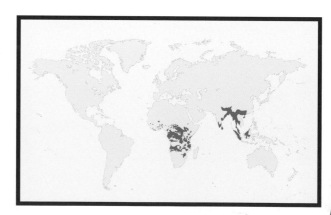

Middle East through Pakistan and India to Indonesia and Borneo, and north into China.

Farms or elephants?

Clearing the land to grow crops and build houses (habitat destruction) has reduced the area in which both African and Asian elephants can live. Hunting has also reduced the ranges of both species. However, they are still fairly widespread.

The African elephant still lives in 36 of Africa's 48 countries. In Asia east of Pakistan the Asian elephant lives in parts of every country apart from Taiwan, Korea, Japan and the Philippines.

The forests where Asian elephants live are often needed for farmland. Each year there is less land for the elephants.

A herd of African elephants near the great peak of Kilimanjaro in Tanzania, eastern Africa.

People and elephants

People and elephants have worked closely together for thousands of years. The Asian elephant in particular has a long history with humans.

Elephants are intelligent animals and can be trained to do all sorts of things. In the past huge numbers of Asian elephants were used in the logging industry. Despite the development of bulldozers and other machinery, thousands of elephants are still used today. The elephant's combination of great strength and nimble feet make it ideal for this heavy work.

⬇ **An elephant at the Songkran festival in Bangkok, Thailand, squirts water over some surprised onlookers.**

Hannibal's elephants

The African elephant is almost unknown as a domestic animal, and many people believe that it cannot be tamed. However, records show that as long ago as 217 B.C. African forest elephants were used as beasts of war. The famous Carthaginian leader Hannibal used the elephants to cross the mountains of the Alps in Europe.

Elephants in zoos

In the western world today elephants are seen mostly in zoos and circuses. Keeping elephants properly requires lots of space, which is something that most zoos and circuses do not have.

⬆ Asian elephants are put to work hauling logs in the logging industry. These elephants in Thailand are giving a demonstration of their amazing strength.

India's elephants

Of all the countries in the world, India has the closest ties to elephants. They are painted and ridden in processions and festivals. They carry tourists through national parks and roam wild in forests. The Hindu religion says they even live in the heavens.

Glossary

ancestors Animals from which elephants have developed over a very long period of time.

bull elephant An adult male elephant.

habitat The kinds of places where a particular animal lives, such as a forest or a desert.

herd A group of elephants. Most herds are made up of related females and their young, but males sometimes form their own herds. A super herd is a collection of many elephants from several herds that meet where there is lots of food to eat. A super herd contains both male and female elephants.

infrasound Noises that are too low-pitched for humans to hear but which can be made and heard by elephants.

mammal A kind of animal that is warm-blooded and has a backbone. Most mammals are covered with fur.

Female mammals have glands that produce milk to feed their young.

matriarch The oldest and largest female; the leader of the herd.

molar A large tooth used for grinding.

must A temporary change in the behaviour of adult male elephants that makes them more aggressive.

testosterone A chemical called a hormone that bull elephants produce when they go into must.

trumpeting The loud noise made by elephants.

trunk A combination of an elephant's nose and upper lip. It is used to pick up food, suck up water, and to smell.

tusk Two giant teeth at the front of the mouth used for digging, pulling and fighting. Elephants are still hunted for their valuable ivory tusks, although the practice is illegal.

Further Reading

Books

Baby Elephant. Ginjer Clarke. London: Penguin, 2009.

Elephant (Eyewitness). Ian Redmond. London: Dorling Kindersley, 2000.

Elephants. Francis Brennan. New York: Children's Press, 2012.

Elephants. Kate Davies. London: Usborne, 2009.

Elephants. Paul May. Oxford: Oxford University Press, 2009.

Great Migrations: Elephants. Marilyn Courtot. Washington, D.C.: National Geographic, 2010.

World of Animals. Susannah Davidson. London: Usborne, 2013.

Websites

BBC Nature
Elephants videos, news and facts.
www.bbc.co.uk/nature/life /Elephantidae

African Elephants
Learn all you want to know about African elephants with pictures, videos, facts and news from National Geographic.
animals.nationalgeographic.co.uk /animals/African-elephant

Elephant Encyclopedia
Facts and general information about elephants.
www.elephant.se

The Worldwide Fund for Nature
Topical information about elephant conservation in Africa and Asia.
www.panda.org

African Wildlife Foundation
Conservation projects for elephants and other African animals.
www.awf.org

EleAid
Lots of information about elephants and a great photo album.
www.eleaid.com

Index